In Him and through Him

All Scriptures quoted are taken from the King James version unless stated otherwise.

Dear Reader

You are a treasure, you are a pearl of great price, you are loved, you are unique, you are who God created you to be. Embrace yourself, love yourself.

Above all remember God loves YOU.

In Him and through Him

Contents

In the arms of....

When a person whether male or female is suffering for example from domestic violence, they often flea from their home or country and seek shelter at a refuge. According to the internet a refuge is a place or state of safety. Those fleeing from domestic violence want to go to a place where they know they are safe, where they are protected, shielded from any danger. Whilst you are inside the refuge then you are safe. The moment you step outside of it you are not. However, you need to go to the refuge in the first place and no one is turned away in their time of need. The refuge also needs to be accessible as otherwise there is no use of it.

 It got me thinking that Christ can be seen as a refuge and is a refuge for all. He is accessible, you are safe in Him, He will protect you, He will not turn you away. If you remain in Christ then you are safe, if you leave Him you are exposed to the dangers of the world

I read on the internet that Christ is a refuge for all sorts of sinners; these people were in a kind of exile who fled to refuges, but in Christ is complete liberty.

The following scriptures are just a reminder that God is our refuge and we can take comfort in that.

Psalm 46:1 says God is our refuge and strength, a very present help in time of trouble.

Deuteronomy 33:27 the Eternal God is your refuge and in 2 Samuel 22:31 it says He is a shield to all who take refuge in Him.

Be blessed today. Why not make God your refuge? He is waiting with open arms.

Point of view

I was on my Facebook page on Saturday and there was this new change they had made, when I go onto my page 'I'm not perfect but that's ok' I now have the option to view my page from my audiences' point of view. I can see what they see. It's made me realise how I see my page is different to what my audience sees, and it enables me to see if I need to make any changes, I can work out is my page appealing to them, does it attract them, am I keeping them engaged. Do they like what they see.

It got me thinking, there is a saying that goes 'beauty is in the eye of the beholder' and how I see myself is not how God sees me, He sees me from his perspective and angle. He sees me as being fearfully and wonderfully made, He sees me as a conqueror. He sees me as His daughter. God sees so much more than I can see. God knows that what He sees is appealing to Him, there's nothing physical about me that He wants to change. When I look at myself from my perspective, I see something different. I struggle to see the beautiful person God has declared and designed me to be. I struggle sometimes to know that I am more than a conqueror. But, as God is the beholder of me, then I am beautiful.

Mirrors can give a reflection of your image, but mirrors aren't always 100% correct, if the lighting is bad it may give a different image i.e. it may make me look darker or my face fatter. We don't always have an accurate view of ourselves. It's a challenge for me to see myself from God's view and it's a challenge I am slowly trying to work on.

Be blessed today as we learn to see ourselves from God's perspective.

Hear my cry

As a mother I have had plenty experience of a child crying. When my son was first born anytime he cried I instantly picked him up, needless to say over the months this habit became less. It took me a while to learn that not every cry meant I needed to hold him. According to the net I found 9 different reasons why a baby may cry (although there may be more), these were: wind, hunger, gas, discomfort, pain, tiredness, fussiness, boredom or to be held.

It got me thinking there are times when all I can do is cry, whether it be to God, myself or another person. It's all I can do at that time to communicate. Whilst some may not understand the reason for my crying, God does, He recognises my pain and what I am crying for, He holds me. Sometimes I cry out because I am tired- tired of being in the same situation, or I'm hungry- hungry for the word of God or the Holy

Spirit, or for more of God's Grace and Mercy, when I feel totally helpless. Or I may just cry because I need God or someone to just hold me or it's a cry of desperation/deliverance.

Sometimes it is hard to cry to God, but it says in *Psalm 61:1-2 Hear MY cry oh Lord, attend unto MY prayer. From the ends of the earth will I cry unto thee.*

Do you need to cry unto God today? Its ok if you do, He is waiting to wipe your tears away.

Suicide prevention day

When people look at you externally and see what you have got and/or achieved, many find it difficult to understand why you would want to kill yourself. Having material things does not always replace the emotional needs, the loneliness, the struggles. As a Christian many also may not understand why you feel suicide is the answer and scriptures are then quoted at you. people become suicidal for a variety of reasons, many may know that it is not the answer, but when you are going through something that pains you, consumes you, eats you, you've cried, you've talked, you've cried some more yet the pain is unbearable, nothing or no one can take it away. Then yes death becomes the solution, just imaging the pain going or the fact that you will no longer have to feel lonely, you pop those pills one by one. I talk from experience, I talk from experience of trying three times. I talk from experience of still experiencing suicidal thoughts and ideations, I talk from experience of the struggle of not taking paracetamols for a headache for fear of taking them all, I talk from experience of spending the day planning my death.

Telling someone they are selfish, or you'll be ok or stay strong doesn't always help a person at that time, so what can we do to help someone who feels suicidal.

Today 10 September 2020 is world suicide prevention day. It is no respecter of persons. How can we help each other?

If you need help you can contact Samaritans on 116 123 day or night.

Promises

My son seemed to be ever so convincing and I even think he convinced himself when he said, "I promise I will wash up today", he even threw in a couple hand gestures for reassurance. Hence 24 hours later his promise was nil and void.

 He had not kept it and I was disappointed in myself for believing him. Sometimes over the years we may have promised things to other people with every good intention of keeping it, some promises we may follow through, others not. Imagine you lend someone some money and they say I promise I will pay you back in a week and so you make plans for that money, when the time comes they have a reason why they can't pay you, you're disappointed in them, saying to yourself you will never borrow them money again. They let you down.

 It got me thinking, when God promises us something, there is no disappointment, no let down.

God is not a man that He should lie, in *Psalms 89:34 it says "no, I will not break my covenant, I will not take back one word of what I said" (TLB version)* and *in 2 Corinthians 1:20 "for ALL the promises of God in Him are yes and in Him amen"(NKJV)*

The last scripture states ALL the promises, not some, not a few, not one, but ALL the promises.

We have been promised eternal life... *1 John 2:25*

There is a song that goes 'Standing on the promises of Christ my King, through eternal ages let His praises ring, gory in the highest, I will shout and sing, standing on the promises of God'

Be blessed today as you continue to stand on the promises of God.

Under attack

Wednesday I went to the cinema and watched the new fast and furious film. There was one part in the film where one of the CIA agents opened a door and was faced with at least 10 bad guys all armed. He took a deep breath and entered the room and one by one the bad guys started to attack him, some came from behind, some jumped on him, at one stage the CIA agent was fighting 3 bad guys at one time, long story short he managed to defeat them all and carried on with his task.

It got me thinking, sometimes in life pressures, trials, illness, financial problems, ups and downs can attack us at the same time and we don't know which one to deal with first, just like the agent we sometimes may deal with one issue and creeping up behind is another issue and we may feel outnumbered. But the scripture *Psalms 91:7 reminds us that a thousand may fall at your side,*
And ten thousand at your right hand;
But it shall not come nigh you.

These last few weeks have felt like the fiery darts have been aimed straight at me and my mind has been attacking me left, right and centre but God has kept me through.

Be blessed today as even though you may feel or be under attack God will deliver and bring you through.

Contractual hours

Some of us have full time jobs, some part time, some zero-hour contract, some term time workers only. We kind of work the hours that are suitable to our lifestyle, occasionally it may be due to the fact you cannot get any other hours, but I am going on the premise that it is suitable for our lifestyle.

For example, a seasonal worker may only work during the Christmas period and a zero-hour contract worker works as and when the need arises.

It got me thinking, am I like that with my relationship with God, am I a seasonal Christian whereby I only acknowledge God in the good times or am I a zero-hour Christian where I just acknowledge God when I want or need something.

A part time worker does not get paid a full-time wage, a zero-hour contract worker does not get paid for hours not worked.

God is not a part time God and even when we do not give God ourselves full time, He still provides, still gives, still makes a way, He doesn't say ok Michelle you didn't pray today so I won't give you any of my Mercy today or I won't cover you with my blood today. How great is our God!!

God always desires 100% of us, I speak to myself first as I know should be doing better.

Be blessed today.

Helmet of....

When cycling, riding a motorbike, a horse or even boxing we wear a helmet to protect our head.

The purpose of a helmet is to absorb the force, which protects your head, which in turn protects your brain. Helmets work to prevent head injuries.

When we put the helmet on in the above scenarios, we need to keep it on otherwise it will be of no use to us. When getting ready to fight in a battlefield, the helmet is the last piece of armour to be put on, without it the armour suite is incomplete.

It got me thinking putting on the helmet is a physical thing, it requires an action from us, and the same way we need to physically put on the helmet, we need to do so in the spiritual.

In ***Ephesians 6:17 it speaks of taking the helmet of Salvation***. The word take means to reach for and hold, to acquire. We need to take hold of the salvation we have received.

Salvation is saving the soul from sin and its consequences salvation is not a onetime thing, we need to do it daily, we need to protect our mind, our thoughts, there is a book by Joyce Meyer entitled the mind is a battlefield. Therefore, we need to guard and protect our mind by something strong that can withstand force. We need to protect what can enter our mind. Each day we need to spiritually put on the helmet of salvation.

Be blessed today.

Firm foundation

I like watching programmes like grand designs, I like to see the finished product. Imagine, the house begins as an idea in someone's mind, then that idea gets drawn by an architect, the foundation is then laid, the bricks are built and before you know you have the house. what got to me is that a house can't be built in one day. You may have an idea of the house and may even have the plans drawn up, but those plans could lay for years until you have the money to make it happen.

Sometimes in the programme, the building gets started and half way through the builders hit problems, the builder's run off, more money is needed, an unexpected fault is found, it very rarely runs smooth.

The most important part I have learned whilst watching these programmes is that the foundation needs to be laid first. It must be a firm foundation, a strong foundation so that any weight added to it can withhold.

Sometimes in life it feels like my foundation is weak and any problem or trial and it causes me to crumble. It's a bit like a man who built his house on the sand, the rain came and washed it away. The house may have looked pretty but the minute a storm came, as there was no foundation, it could not withstand. It got me thinking, is my foundation strong, what is my foundation, and who is my foundation.

This week has been difficult, well, the last few months have been, and I felt like my foundation was beginning to crumble and at the slightest problem I was ready to give up, my foundation wasn't strong enough to hold on. But if Christ is my foundation and Solid Rock then I should be able to stand. I need to make Christ my foundation and stand upon Him and Him only, as the song says, 'on Christ the Solid Rock I stand, all other ground is sinking sand'. And we all know what sinking sand can do, it can kill us as it cannot support weight.

Pray for me saints, I need to get out of the sinking sand.

Wash day

Saturday was the day my hair needed washing. usually, I just wash it when I am in the shower, but, as I had had my hair in a style called kinky twists (which involved gel being applied to my hair) when I was taking them out, I noticed my hair was very thick and dry due to the gel. I was dreading washing it as I knew it was going to be more difficult to manage than usual. The task daunted me.

Then I had the idea of parting my hair into two sections and wash one section at a time, I've never done that before so wasn't sure if it would work, however, it was the best idea at the time. To be fair I can't believe I've never used that idea before, I took my time on each section, combing my hair through to make sure there were no knots. By the time I had finished I was happy, the task I was dreading turned out to be fine.

It got me thinking, sometimes we may be going through something and looking at it and wondering how I am going to get through/deal with this. Just like with my hair, maybe we could look at the issue/problem and take just one section of it and deal with it. Then, we can move on to the next section and deal with it, so piece by piece we are dealing with our issue but in a more manageable way.

Be blessed today

Right angle

Whenever I look down at my stomach it always looks big, but, if I turn to the side and look at it sideways it gives me a different outlook, it doesn't look as fat. And sometimes when I believe it is fat another person says stop being silly, your stomach is not big, they say that because that is there outlook on it.

 It got me thinking, sometimes I may look at my problems from an incorrect angle and the problem seems bigger than what it is, but, if I don't change my position then it will always seem big. Or, have you ever watched a programme where someone has caught a fish and the next day they are asked how big the fish was, and they stretch out there arms to make it seem like it was a gigantic fish, when, in reality it was the size of a sprat. I suppose what I'm saying is, sometimes we may exaggerate/amplify the size of our problem, don't get me wrong, at the time when we are going through it may seem large, but, if we just took a step back and looked at the size of our God then the size of our problem will seem relatively small. We mustn't look at the size of our problems and think God this is too big for you, let me turn to drink instead, no, we need to turn to God, who is our refuge and a very present help in time of trouble. We serve a God who is Omnipotent. **There Is Nothing Too Difficult For Him.**

 We mustn't limit the size of our problems to a God is who is not constrained by concepts or limitations.

 Be blessed today as I leave you with the following scriptures.

Behold, I am the Lord, the God of all flesh. Is there anything too hard for me? (Jeremiah 32:27).

 But Jesus looked at them and said, "For mortals it is impossible, but for God all things are possible" (Matthew 19:26).

Walk of witness

Good Friday was the first time I had taken part in the walk of witness for a good few years. I had tried to get out of it, but my pastor told me no lol. Anyway, as I was walking (which may have been around 2 miles) with nothing in my hands, the sun was hot and I felt drained, I had no water and only a couple of sweets and I said to my friend how I tired I was and needed to sit down and unsure if I can finish the walk.

It got me thinking as I thought about Jesus carrying His cross and our sins all the way to Calvary. I don't know how many miles it was, but I guarantee it wasn't two. Bearing in mind He had been beaten, whipped and bruised AND then made to carry a cross of unbearable weight. Did Jesus moan once... no, did He complain once.... no. Can you imagine how much the weight of carrying our sins were? For a sinless man to become laden with our sin so that we could be free.

I don't know what the weather was like but if it was hot like it was on Good Friday, He must have been more than suffering.

I soon stopped moaning about the little walk I made and put things into perspective. Jesus knew from His birth that this day would come, it didn't make it any easier for Him, He didn't disappear when the time came, He didn't come up with an alternative. No, He was obedient unto the point of death.

Be blessed today as we continue to reflect on the sacrifice made for us.

Mother's Day Pain

Yesterday around 7pm I was laying in my bed and the tears I had been fighting all day finally came, however, I couldn't allow myself to cry for long because it would just make it real, I mean, it's already real, but if I cried, it would be really real. I'd spent all day shutting myself off from emotions, from any messages I received. I was ok until I got to Morrison's and saw loads of people picking up bunches of flowers, chocolates, plants etc. and jealousy, anger and sadness hit me. I tried to sing a song so that I wouldn't be angry at God, but, if I'm honest, I was upset with Him.

 Then it was all the Facebook and Instagram posts with pictures of people's mothers and lovely sentiments and again I got angry. Angry that I have no pictures, angry that I have no memories or to be even able to say happy Mother's Day to the world's best mom. No memories to get me through the day, just a deep longing and void that wasn't going to be filled. I thought about those whose first Mother's Day this is without their mother, or a mother without their child, I thought about my son, I thought God when Mother's Day will ever be bearable for me. I thought God what lesson are you teaching me and questioned if I haven't I learnt it yet.

I leave you with the words from a song by Donald Lawrence. Something that I had to do yesterday to make it to today

"Sometimes you have to encourage yourself, sometimes you have to speak victory during the test, and no matter how you feel, speak the word and you will be healed, speak over yourself, encourage yourself in the Lord."

Tatoes

I love potatoes, mashed, fried, baked, boiled, roasted, chips, jacket potatoes, crisps lol, I love potatoes. However, I am not entirely sure they agree with my digestive system as it sometimes seems to irritate or flair up my IBS.

But because I love how they taste I continue to eat them knowing they may be doing me more harm than good.

It got me thinking, sometimes we may like to hear preaching that is not biblically correct but because we like how it tastes or it tastes good because we are not living a lifestyle pleasing to God, we continue to hear the preaching and let it in our spiritual digestive system and cause us eternal damage.

Another food that doesn't agree with me is bread, especially white bread, when I eat it, it makes me feel bloated and causes cramps, but, I have however found a bread that no matter how much I eat of it, it doesn't not make me feel unwell, this bread is found in **John 6:35**

Then Jesus declared, "I am the bread of life". This is the bread that we all need to eat, in *Matthew 26:26 Jesus took bread, and after blessing it broke it and gave it to the disciples, and said, "Take, eat; this is my body*". This is an instruction from Jesus to eat bread, bread that will satisfy our soul and hunger.

Be blessed today as we continue to do what it says in *John 6:27... Do not work for food that spoils, but for food that endures to eternal life, which the Son of Man will give you. For on him God the Father has placed his seal of approval.*"

Stand still

Most competitors in a race enter with either one or two outcomes in mind, one is to win the race and two is to just finish the race. They don't get to the start line and think to themselves I'll only run so far and quit, during the race/marathon they may become tired, legs may begin to hurt and they feel like quitting but someone on the side line or finish line is cheering them on, encouraging them, or, they can see the finish line ahead of them and it spurs them on to continue.

I have seen on occasions where someone is running a marathon and for whatever reason they become disorientated or fall over and another runner/competitor has stopped and helped this person. The person who helped may have been in the lead and ready to be the first to cross the finish line, but, to them, making sure another person finishes the race is more important to them.

It got me thinking, sometimes in life it can feel like that, we all want to finish the race and make heaven our home, and likewise, if we see someone stumble, fall, struggling, we should be helping them too so that they can finish the race with us. Or, we need to encourage our family/friends who are on the side-lines to come and join in the race with us.

Most prizes given when you have won a race are medals, certificates or trophies, we too will receive a prize at the end as stated in **1 Corinthians 9:24-25 *Do you not know that in a race all the runners run, but only one receives the prize? So, run that you may obtain it. Every athlete exercises self-control in all things. They do it to receive a perishable wreath, but we an imperishable wreath.***

Every race has their rules and if you don't follow them, you may be disqualified. Have you seen where winners have been stripped of their title and/or medal? According **to 2 Timothy 2:5 *An athlete is not crowned unless he competes according to the rules, our aim is that crown***.

Be blessed today as we strive to be able to ***say I have fought the good fight, I have finished the race, I have kept the faith (2 Timothy 4:7)***

Storm Manuel

Imagine, there's storm Manuel hitting your area, you feel brave enough to pop out to get some milk and a piece of wind suddenly comes and tries to knock you over. You do all you can to avoid this, you may turn your back to the wind, may cling on to something, may place your feet in a different position because come what may, the storm cannot knock you over. It may take all your strength, may take all your energy but you will not be knocked over.

This last couple weeks it felt like a storm has been hitting me emotionally and mentally, it tried to knock me over, tried to take me out. I've tried to stand, tried to plant my feet firmly on the Solid Rock. It felt at times that I could feel the emotional storm start making me sway, I even bent over with the force but somehow through it all I didn't fall over, it didn't knock me down completely.

In 2 Corinthians 4: 9 it says We are hunted

down, but never abandoned by God. We get

knocked down, but we are not destroyed.

There is a song by Deitrick Haddon that goes.

'Stand still and know that He is God, and there's no need to fight, the battle is not yours, the battle is the Lord's.'

This reminds me that whatever our battle may be, emotionally, physically, spiritually etc., we just need to stand still and know that the battle is the Lord's, and God does not and cannot lose the fight.

Be blessed today.

Praise constipation

One of the side effects of not having enough water or fibre in your diet or eating a lot of dairy products, lack of exercise and stress can result in us suffering from constipation. And we know the struggle when you are constipated, you have the urge, but nothing comes out (sorry to sound crude).

It got me thinking. Sometimes it feels like I have a praise and worship constipation in the sense that there is something that prevents me from praising or worshipping. The praise is there but for some reason I cannot let it come out. Last week at church the pastor done an altar call for those who felt their praise had gone, I went up for prayer and I lifted my hands but the worship that I wanted to come out was not coming out. I struggled, the worship was there, but I did not know how to release it. I got frustrated with myself.

I need to find out what it is that is preventing me from praising God, because constant praise constipation is not good for me spiritually.

There's a song by J Moss that goes 'There's a praise on the inside I can't keep to myself, a holler stirring up from the depths of my soul'

This is my desire. keep me in your prayers please.

When I am weak

One evening last year I decided to take a bite from a chocolate I brought. I went to bite the chocolate using my side tooth and the chocolate was a bit hard and as I went to bite down my tooth fell out. I was vexed because I didn't even need to eat the chocolate as I wasn't even that hungry.

I didn't seem too concerned as I had kept the tooth and was under the impression the dentist could just pop it back in.

Well, my trip to the dentist cost me £400!!! The tooth had to be replaced.

It got me thinking, sometimes when we think we are strong, the simplest trial, situation etc. comes our way and we sink, we crumble, we fall. Just like my tooth. I had no reason to think that it would fall out, it gave no warning sign, wasn't loose or wobbling and had been functioning fine until that moment.

Sometimes I think I am strong and that I can face the battle when actually I am weak. I have not prayed enough, read enough or spent time seeking God. On the outside I look strong, but when push comes to shove, I crumble. It reminds me of the scripture in **2 Corinthians 12:10 that says, "for when I am weak, then I am strong".** Sometimes we need to become weak so that God's strength can be shown in us, we move from doing it ourselves to letting God do it. when we rely on God, we move from our imperfect strength to Gods perfect strength. When we rely on God at our weakest point, we become perfected.

This last couple of weeks it is God's strength that has kept me, I had to step back and say God I need you, I cannot do this by myself.

As we continue in this new year let God be your strength, let Him be your perfect strength. When He is our strength we cannot fail.

Be blessed today.

Force ripe

Something my pastor preached on Sunday and I had to share again. He said you can have ripe, and you can have force ripe. We know when a mango has been allowed to ripen by itself and when it's been force ripe. When it's been force ripe, they look the same, but the taste is different. It lacks the sweetness that it should have because the sugars have not had time to mature. So whilst it looks big it tends to have no taste. Some of us are going through some things that are tasteless because we are trying to hurry God in the midst of what He is doing with us. God said I'm bringing you to maturity and we say God I want it now. God says I'm taking you through and you say God take me through now and sometimes God says ok I will bring you through now, and we don't like the taste, we say God why is my situation still like this, why is it worse than when I went in. God said I already told you **they that wait upon me shall renew their strength, they will mount with wings like eagles, if you wait on Me you will not give up**

because you will walk and not faint. Teach me Lord to wait.

Partially quoted from Isaiah 40:31

Trust God

I've been playing this game for around 3 months now on my phone, I haven't got a clue what the game is about or what I am supposed to collect and why, but I continue to find the hidden items and hope for the best. I know there is some logic to the game, but I have not found it or understood it. I continue to play the game blindly because I enjoy it and like looking forward to the next level. Then there are times when I am playing a different game and I have nearly completed the level and I get frustrated because I'm not winning but I carry on because I need to finish, I need to move to the next level. Then there are some games where aids are given in order to help me complete that level and believe me they come in handy.

 It got me thinking, sometimes I find this happens in my Christian faith, I sometimes feel as If I don't know what I'm doing or why but I continue to carry on because it will make sense at some point, according to **Proverbs 3:5-6** it tells me to *Trust in the LORD with all your heart, and do not lean on your own understanding. In all your ways acknowledge him, and he will make straight your paths*. So therefore, I carry on regardless as I know there will be an expected outcome, I know there will be a point. I may just not understand it at that time. When I feel like giving up, I have to perceiver, it may look like I'm not going to win the battle or that level, but I must give it all that I have and try.

It may be a temporary blip of uncertainty as to if what I am doing is correct or not, it may last a day, it may last a month, but the key word is TEMPORARY.

Just like in the games where I am given aids to help me win, God has given me aids, He has given me His word, the Holy Spirit, prayer, friends, pastors etc. I just need to learn to use them.

Be blessed today as we are reminded in *Jeremiah 29:11 that God knows the plans He has for us, plans for welfare and not for evil, to give you a future and a hope.*

Let there be light

I was talking to my pastor about something, and I said I feel it's dark in my life and he replied darkness is just the absence of light, and the moment you can see any light it's no longer dark. Once we see a flicker of light, it's our focus on that light that will guide us to where we need to be. A bit like a lighthouse guiding the ships, it serves as a navigational guide to steer ships but the light needs to be situated high enough to be seen before the danger is reached by a mariner, and the mariner needs to look out for the light and be guided by it.

We don't measure darkness, we measure the amount of light there is. When we are facing our darkness, we need to look to Jesus for He is the light of the world and be guided by Him. We were never designed to live in darkness completely, remember God said let there be light!

Trust

When we are in labour, we trust that the midwife will deliver our baby safely, when we order an item from the internet, we expect the postman or courier to deliver the item, when we order a take-away we expect the food to be delivered. We put our trust in these people.

If we can trust the qualified, why do we sometimes not trust the one who qualified these people. We take the word of a midwife or a certificate and trust they will deliver a baby safely, we take the word of a pilot that he will land/deliver us to our destination, we don't question them, we don't doubt them.

It got me thinking, if I can trust these people, then why do I find it hard to trust that God will deliver me in times of trouble.

In 2 Samuel 22:2-3 it states that the Lord is our rock, fortress and my DELIVERER!!!

What more evidence or proof do I need.

The following scriptures all speak about deliverance

Psalm 34:4 I sought the LORD, and he answered me; he delivered me from all my fears.

Psalm 34:17 The righteous cry out, and the LORD hears them; he delivers them from all their troubles.

Psalm 50:15 And call upon me in the day of trouble; I will deliver you, and you shall glorify me.

Psalm 107:19, Then they cried to the LORD in their trouble, and he delivered them from their distress. (English Standard Version)

2 Timothy 4:18, Yes, and the Lord will deliver me from every evil attack and will bring me safely into his heavenly Kingdom. All glory to God forever and ever! Amen. **(New Living Translation Version)**

We even pray in the Lord's prayer for God to deliver us from evil, therefore we need to take assurance that when we pray this that He will indeed deliver us, deliver us from whatever we ask for.

Be blessed today as we trust that God can and will deliver us.

Mental health

When someone can spend the morning laughing and talking with you and by the evening you have heard they have killed themselves, when you ask someone repeatedly if they are ok and they smile and reply I'm fine and then the next day you hear they killed themselves. Or you see them at church worshipping and by Sunday evening message sent saying they have died. Or you tell someone that if they ever need to talk, they can call you, then you receive a phone call saying that committed suicide.

 When you feel suicidal, sometimes no matter how many people say they are there for you, you feel alone, you feel no-one understands or can feel the immense pain you are in, for that person life is so unbearable that they cannot contemplate that life is worth living, they are battling their demons and they lost the battle. Many don't understand why people commit suicide and say that person is selfish, they didn't try hard enough etc., but it is a battle of the mind, a mental illness, sometimes the person may not even want those suicidal thoughts, but they have them.

 For me as a Christian who has struggled with those thoughts for years and acted on them, how do we seek help, how do we help another Christian in the same boat, we all know killing ourselves is a sin and that alone people would think would stop us, but, imagine your desperate for the toilet and you have held it in for as long as possible until you can no longer hold it in. that's what feeling suicidal can be like. How do you explain to another Christian that you hate life and they quote scriptures at you, how do you explain to another Christian you want to die and they quote but Jesus died so you can live, how do you tell another Christian you are in so much pain that suicide is the only way out and they refuse to talk to you again.

I saw a post on Facebook where a young musician, gifted musician took his own life, in every picture he looked happy, who knew the demons he faced. Behind the smiles can be anguish, heartache, pain, loneliness.

 Suicide is real and is real for many Christians...... We need to share our stories so we can help someone else

Expectancy

When we are pregnant we wait with expectancy, when we get a promotion we wait in expectancy, when we get engaged we wait with expectancy, when we go to a concert we wait with expectancy for the artist to come on stage, when we are at the bus stop we wait with expectancy, when it is pay day we wait with expectancy, we wait expecting an outcome, we wait expecting something. At the women's empowerment conference last week, the guest speaker Rev Jennifer Porter-Cox said we must worship in expectancy, to me this means that whatever we have prayed for, asked for, requested, in the waiting season we must worship with the expectation that we will receive.

 Noah waited with expectancy when he built the ark, Jacob waited in expectancy for Rachel, Abraham waited in expectation of a child, john the Baptist waited in expectation of He who should come after him.

In the waiting period the above people carried on working, carried on trusting in God, when the people laughed at Noah for building an ark, he carried on building it, He trusted and believed God.

Habakkuk 2:3 For the vision is yet for an appointed time; But at the end it will speak, and it will not lie. Though it tarries, wait for it; Because it will surely come, It will not tarry.

To tarry means to linger in expectation, to wait in expectation for the vision, for your vision, for the promises God has made to you.

Be blessed today

Fit for nothing

When TK Maxx have their final clearance sale on I get very excited, that is until I pick up some of the items and noticed they are damaged and have flaws in them, pieces are missing, so I throw them back down in disgust and question how can they sell broken goods, or, have you ever picked up a banana and its bruised and battered and in your eyes not fit for human consumption.

It got me thinking, sometimes we may look at people and because of their current or past lifestyle we may think they are damaged goods and discard them from our lives as they obviously have nothing they can offer. I have been reading the book of Ruth and noticed that Boaz married Ruth who was a Moabites (the Moab's were products of incest and Boaz in effect shouldn't have married her), but, when we look further in the bible and the lineage of Jesus, we see Ruth in there. There are five women in the lineage of Jesus who in the eyes of people at the time, had no right to be in there.

Bathsheba was an adulteress, Rahab was a prostitute (also Boaz's grandmother), Tamar was pregnant by her father in law, Ruth came from a banned nation and Mary was unwed when she became pregnant.

But it shows that God looked beyond that and saw it fit that His Son should be brought forth through these damaged people. The lineage of Jesus can be seen as the story of redemption.

As Bishop John Jackson preached once, God is a regarder of the disregarded.

Be blessed today

Urgency

There have been times when my son wants me to do something for him and its urgent and needs to be done now now now, but, when I ask him to do something, he's reply is what's the rush, it's not urgent.

My son and I both have different ideas of what requires urgency or not, me asking him to wash the dishes and 1 week later there still unwashed, he still doesn't see the need to get a move on, but if I don't transfer some money into his account 2 minutes after he has asked me it's a crisis.

It got me thinking, sometimes it's a bit like that with me and God, I may be asking God for example for a husband and I'm like it's an urgent need and I need a husband now and God is saying yeah it can wait, it's not as urgent as you think.

There is something though that is very urgent for believers and non-believers, Jesus is returning soon, and we need to make sure that we are right with God as believers and that as non-believers we get to know God and accept Him. There is an urgency in this because we may say I'll do it next week, but, as stated in the scripture **Romans 13:11 Do this, knowing the time, that it is already the hour for you to awaken from sleep; for now salvation is nearer to us than when we believed.**

Be blessed today and seek the Lord while He may be found

I wanna hold your hand

When my son was younger, he used to hold my hand when walking on the street or when crossing the road, as he got older, he held my hand less and less until it stopped completely. He had got too old.

Sometimes I see couples walking along holding their partners hand, or you may have a best friend that you hold hands with, at church we hold hands with the person sitting next to us, we may hold hands with the person who is praying for us.

For me, holding someone's hand brings about a sense of relationship, a bond, a connection, a closeness, they may hold your hand tight, so you feel secure. When I used to hold my sons' hands, I would often hold it tight so he couldn't let go and run off towards danger. I imagined it may have frustrated him, but it may have also felt the love. Sometimes, he would initiate and hold my hand. When someone is in labour, they always show the woman holding the partners hand as a sense of support, comfort.

To hold hands with someone can mean you have a fondness, rapport, respect, concern, trust and perhaps romantic feelings with that person.

It got me thinking, at church we sing a song that goes 'blessed Jesus hold my hand, yes I need thee every hour, through this land, this pilgrim land, by thy saving power, hear my plea, my feeble plea, lord dear lord look down on me, when I kneel in prayer blessed Jesus hold my hand.

We are never too old for Jesus to hold our hand, whatever the situation or circumstance, whatever you may be feeling, let us learn to ask Jesus to hold our hand, sometimes He may hold our hand so tight so that we can't let go. Don't fight it, embrace it.

Be blessed today

Not fit for the pit

A couple of weeks ago bishop has preached on our dreams that have to die, he referenced to Joseph and said that the same people who put Joseph in the pit were the same people who had to lift him out of the pit, some people who put us down are the same people that are going to elevate us. GODS PURPOSE FOR US IS NOT IN THE PIT!

Bishop then went on to say that the Joseph who went down into the pit was not the same Joseph who came out of the pit, a transformation happened. It got me thinking, we are not the same person who took the steps into the baptismal pool, we may have been dirty, sinful, horrible, wicked etc., but the person emerging from the pool is now different. We emerge with power, strength, forgiveness. We emerge as a child of God, a child of the Most High. We may have been submerged poor, but we emerge rich. We submerged dead but emerged alive.

 Gods design was for us the be elevated, for us to mount on wings as eagles and soar, not roam on the ground or slither around, but to soar, to lift our heads. Joseph had to go down into the pit in order to be elevated, Job had to go down into the pit of despair, grief and illness but was elevated to a much higher place. Sometimes the pit may be what we need so that we can be elevated to where God desires and wants us to be.

Have a blessed day

I swear

Have you ever told someone something and sworn them to secrecy and then spend a period of time worrying you can trust them, or, told them something and they promise they will not tell anyone, next thing you know someone knows your business? It can then put you off confiding in people, in trusting in them. I was watching a programme yesterday that involved a lawyer and their client and the lawyer was telling their client to tell them the truth, the client was a bit reluctant but the lawyer then reminded them of the attorney-client privilege, this is only in the United States and it is a "client's right privilege to refuse to disclose and to prevent any other person from disclosing confidential communications between the client and the attorney.

It got me thinking, we have that same kind of privilege too, we have an advocate The word "advocate" means lawyer or one who pleads our cause or case) we can come to Him with anything, with our dirtiest, most shameful sins and we can be assured it goes no further, He will plead our case, He will hear us. And not only can we be assured that He will not tell anyone, once we have told Him, it gets thrown into the sea of forgetfulness. What an awesome God we serve

This scripture is a reminder to us *1 John 2:1-2 My little children, I am writing these things to you so that you may not sin And if anyone sins, we have an Advocate with the Father, Jesus Christ the righteous; and He Himself is the propitiation for our sins; and not for ours only, but also for those of the whole world.*

Be blessed today

I almost let go

Imagine you're watching a film and two people are walking on a cliff edge, one of them tumbles over and as you glance down, you see them gripping the ledge with their hands, you have no rope to haul them back up, you can see their grip is loosening, you panic, you don't know what to do, you can't believe you are just about to watch someone you love die. You tell to hold on, help is coming and just as they are about to let, you reach over, grab them by their arm and pull them back to safety.

It got me thinking, many times I have been on a cliff edge hanging on for dear life, the grip is getting weaker and weaker, my arm is getting tired, my strength is going, then suddenly, I'm pulled back to safety. The cliff edge may be a problem, may be an illness, a trial, an enemy etc., but God stretches out His arm and reaches out to us just at that crucial moment.

There's a song by Kurt Carr that goes "**I almost gave up. I was right at the edge of a break**

**through but couldn't see it.
The devil really had me, But Jesus came and
grabbed me, and He held me close, so I
wouldn't let go. God's mercy kept me, so I
wouldn't let go".**

God doesn't desire us to let go, He doesn't
want us to let go, He is saying to us, just hold on,
I will not let you fall, you may feel you're
strength has gone, but I am God!

Be blessed today as we take hope in the comfort
that God will keep us

Daisy Daisy

When I was younger, I remember trampling on some daisies until they were flattened and beyond chance of continuing to grow, or, there have been times I have stamped on spiders and ants and crushed them to death. There have also been incidents on the news where people have been trampled on and been seriously injured or killed.

The definition of trample is to **step heavily on or crush someone or something:**

Over the past few days there has been a situation that required trampling on, I could stamp on it, I could squish it, but it wouldn't destroy it and there are certain things which need to be destroyed, to be killed

In Luke 10:19 it says I have given you authority to trample on snakes and scorpions and to overcome all the power of the enemy; nothing will harm you and in *Psalm 91:13 You will tread upon the lion and cobra, The young lion and the serpent you will trample down.*

In the scripture it doesn't say I have been given authority to stamp or squish the serpent or lion and it got me thinking, why did God say trample. Well to trample something it usually results in destruction and I need to trample down the things that would try and destroy me, if I don't trample them then they will trample me, they will kill me. God has given me authority to trample down such things so that I can overcome and be an overcomer.

Keep me in your prayers saints and let us start to trample on things that need to be destroyed

Get on board

Over the last couple of years there have been ticket inspectors waiting at bus stops or on trains and then getting on the bus/train and checking that people have a valid ticket. I've seen people jump out of the bus window to avoid the inspector or maybe hide in the toilet or come out with some random excuse as to why they haven't got a ticket. To be fair the train tickets can be expensive but it's still no excuse not to buy one. for those that do get caught they are then given a fine which sometimes can be more than triple the cost of your original fare. you got on board the bus or train when you never had the means to. Just imagine you can't really enjoy your journey because you are constantly looking out for inspectors.

The other day I was travelling with some family on a minibus to Scotland and the amount of baggage that we brought with us was so funny, another family member was going to meet us there as they were travelling by train. When we all met up, she laughed when she saw all our baggage, she asked us how long we think we are holidaying for? as all she had was a rucksack and said travelling by train she couldn't afford to walk with so much baggage.

it got me thinking, we no longer need to try and avoid bus/train inspectors as there is a train that we don't need a ticket. There's a song that goes **'people get ready, there's a train a-coming, you don't need no ticket, you just get on board, so people get ready for the train a-comin, you don't need no baggage, you just get on board.'** All you need is faith!

Faith is our ticket and Jesus has already inspected us and granted us permission to get on board.

Be blessed today as you get ready to get on board.

Broken for use

When a mosaic piece is finished it looks beautiful, however, in order to get to the finished product, the artist may spend hours assembling small pieces of glass or stone together. So, imagine you break a coloured vase, its shattered into tiny pieces and to you it is now useless, it's broken, no longer has any use and you don't have the desire or patience to fix it. But, to an artist, that broken vase is a masterpiece waiting to be created, to them it needed to be broken for them to use it, an unbroken vase is of no use to them. They specialise in broken things. The artist will gather the pieces and have already visualised the result.

Sometimes in life I feel like that broken vase, I'm shattered, my heart is shattered, I've been broken beyond repair, or sometimes feel that I am too much of a pain for others to want to spend time with me to help 'fix' me. But an artist came along, picked up my broken pieces and is painstakingly assembling the pieces into a work of art. The artist doesn't see me as broken, doesn't see me as shattered and useless, He sees me as a warrior, an overcomer, a survivor. He sees me as His child and wants to spend the time restoring me. He has the patience, He has the glue that will hold me together.

In **Psalms 51:16 we are reminded that a broken and contrite spirit, thou wilt not despise, O God."** And in **Psalm 34:18 The Lord is near to the broken-hearted and saves those who are crushed in spirit.**

Be blessed today as we trust God to create something beautiful out of us

Oh come

I saw this video on Facebook and it was about a baby who was born with no arms or legs and was left in an orphanage, eventually a family adopted her, however, whilst watching the video it made me realise just how helpless the child was, they could do nothing for themselves, they could barely lift their head up, they would be reliant on help for the rest of their life.

It got me thinking, God never leaves us helpless, He always sends someone to assist, you may not realise they have come to assist you, it may not be a physical act, it may be a word, a financial gift, a hug, a dinner invite. God can see and know that the situation we are in may leave us feeling helpless, that we can barely lift our head. These last couple weeks I have felt helpless, and I have been wondering God why have you left me feeling like this, why have you left me to pick up my head when it is so burdened and heavy that I can't.

Scriptures such *as Psalm 121:1 I will lift up mine eyes to the hills from whence comes my help, my help comes from the lord, and psalm 42:11 why are you cast down O my soul* and *Hebrews 4:6 let us therefore come boldly to the throne of grace, that we may obtain mercy and find grace to help in the time of need.*

The last scripture is to me an action scripture, it is saying I need to COME and not just come but BOLDLY come to the throne of grace. If I come but come timidly or weak then fear can continue to creep in, but if I come boldly it shows that I am coming in a confident and courageous way.

Be blessed today as you boldly come to the throne of grace in your time of need.

He's still in control

When watching certain films that involve a boat, dinghy or canoe for example, 9 times out of 10 once they reach their destination, and usually it's some beach in the middle of nowhere, they climb out of the boat and in the blink of an eye the boat drifts out to sea. Either they were too slow in tying it up or they didn't tie it securely and now they are trapped.

It got me thinking, if I am not tied securely to Christ, then I am bound to drift away, If I am not tied securely in my prayer life, bible study, church attendance and relationship with Christ, I will drift away. I may think I am tied securely but if after 2 weeks I've not prayed or studied or communed with God, little by little the devil will come in and start to gently drift me away.

I'm not going to lie, these past few weeks have been difficult and I've felt myself drift, but don't feel I have the strength to pull myself back to safe ground, to re-tie myself. I want to be drifted away.

Have you ever seen a person walking their dog and they have this lead that lets the dog walk quite a way in front, but the owner can still draw the dog back by adjusting the lead? The dog probably thinks he has his freedom, but he is still under control of the lead. Or a toddler who has a harness on them, they may be able to walk independently by not holding their parents/care givers hand, but they are still under control. As much as I feel I am drifting away God has me, I don't believe He will let me drift off permanently or too far, I am under His control.

There's a song by Kirk Franklin that goes 'He's still in control, He's sovereign and He knows, just how it feels to be afraid, have folk you love walk away. Be still and know He's still in control.

And the well know song goes "we **have an anchor that keeps our soul, steadfast and sure while the billows roll"**

I'm having to trust God will keep me anchored. I need Him too desperately

Fruit of the day

At our ladies night at church yesterday there were a range of different fruits such as lemons, strawberries, pears, melon etc on the table, we were a bit intrigued as to why they were there and also hunger set in for me lol.

We were then asked individually what fruit we would pick that best describes us, I chose the melon because although it has a hard exterior/shell, once you cut it open it has a soft centre, I have a hard shell on the outside to protect me from being bruised/damaged/hurt. People may see this in a negative way, but, once you open me up (not literally) I have a soft inside, I am loving, caring etc.

If you dropped the melon onto the floor, unlike a strawberry, it won't smash or be squished. Its exterior protects it, you don't know what is inside until you open it. People won't get to know me by just making judgement on my shell. Sometimes we do and I do it myself, when I'm buying fruit sometimes you look at the outside, try and smell if it is sweet and then make a judgment call based on that, sometimes it works, other times it doesn't.

At bible study a couple weeks ago we were looking at the declaration of faith and touched on the fruit of the spirit. Bishop John Jackson asked us how many fruits of the spirit were there and answers ranged from 7 to 9 to 11. But Bishop replied and said there is only one. I looked at him in disbelief, no, there are 9 fruits!!!!

But when I re-read **Galatians 5:22-23 it says but the fruit of the Spirit is**...... doesn't say fruits!

Bishop then went on to give an example of a Satsuma, it is one fruit but once peeled there are different segments to the one fruit. I never viewed it like that, was very eye opening and made me realise that the Satsuma is a whole fruit, we don't go out and buy segments of the fruit, likewise, the fruit of the spirit is one and we should be aiming to have all those different segments in our lives daily.

Galatians 5:22-23 But the fruit of the Spirit is love, joy, peace, forbearance, kindness, goodness, faithfulness, gentleness and self-control. Against such things there is no law. (NIV)

Phantom pain

I've never had a leg or arm amputated, but I have read stories from those who have, and they mention something about phantom pain. according to the internet Phantom limb pain (PLP) refers to ongoing painful sensations that seem to be coming from the part of the limb that is no longer there. The limb is gone, but the pain is real.

It got me thinking, since my mom died, I have experienced pain, it feels as if a part of me has been amputated, the limb is my mother, she has gone but the pain is real. That part of me has gone, it can't be re-grown, can't be reattached.

After amputation some people may be offered/given what is known as a prosthesis-which is an artificial device that replaces a missing body part. Prosthetics are intended to restore the normal functions of the missing body part.

Years ago, the artificial limb was quite basic, you could tell it was artificial and I suppose didn't really offer much use to the person, but it replaced a part of the body that was missing, nowadays, technology has developed and some of the limbs are mid blowing. It takes the person a while to get used to the limb and how to function it and accept it as part of their body.

I have had people in my life over the years who have become like a mother to me, who have replaced my missing limb- my mother, just like the above scenario it has taken me a while to accept that these 'mothers' love me and want to be a part of my life and accept me.

Today is a difficult day, a very lonely day, a very reflective day, a day when I wish my 'limb was never amputated'.

God says He will never give us more than we can bear and today I need His strength.

Never grow weary

In this current heatwave, the sun has knocked me out, I remember walking into town on my lunch breaks and because of the heat I felt faint, I felt weary, I was dragging myself along, I just never had any energy, or, when I was at the gym (when I used to try and keep fit) I would go on the treadmill for say half an hour, but after 10 mins of running I grew tired, I hadn't the strength to carry on running, so my running became walking and my walking became a stroll until eventually out of tiredness I gave up.

It got me thinking, in life we are bound to feel weary, feel faint, feel weak. Even athletes must grow weary during a marathon or 1000m run, but, even if they do they persevere, sometimes in a race you see the athletes sprint off so fast that after the first lap they are tired, whereas you may get other athletes who start off slow, but as they see the finish line approaching, they gather their strength and take first place.

There's been times in my spiritual walk that I have grown tired, don't have the strength, feel like I've walked or come as far as I can go, but the song reminds me that **I can't give up now, I've come to far from where I started from.**

Just like the athlete above who has ran 9990m out of 1000m and thinks, I can't give up now, I ran too far, I've walked to far, he pushes himself, he knows he needs to carry on, he may stop temporarily and refresh himself, may stop temporarily to gather more strength, but he stops in order to keep going. Sometimes we have to stop fighting, stop using our own strength, stop and be renewed, stop and let God be our strength, stop and let Him fight our battles, stop and wait on the lord, stop and hope in the lord, THEN, we will not grow weary, nor faint, but SOAR.

But those who hope in the LORD will renew their strength. They will soar on wings like eagles; they will run and not grow weary, they will walk and not be faint. Isaiah 40:13

Lost but found

I remember years ago I was in town with my son and he ran off into a shop, one minute he was walking beside me and the next he'd gone, the panic and fear that I felt was indescribable. I couldn't find him, I called his name, I searched the shop and even asked staff if they had seen him.

Or there has been times when I'm at a shopping mall trying to meet up with someone, I can't find them, so I ring and get their location but still can't find them, and panic sets in.

Lately, I have been feeling lost, feeling God has left me, like the example with my son, it felt one-minute God was walking beside me and then suddenly He had gone, I called out to God, I searched for Him, but I couldn't find Him, I felt alone, abandoned.

It got me thinking, God never leaves us, we may leave Him, but He never forsakes us. When my son ran off, it was him who left my side, it was him who made the move, I hadn't gone nowhere, I hadn't left him. He left me.

I remember on Friday feeling terribly alone and people were saying you are never alone, God is always with you. I didn't want to hear it because I couldn't feel it. I couldn't feel Him. But, if we are to walk by faith and not by sight then I have to believe that when God says ' Lo I am with you always' then that is what He means, not I am with you sometimes, or only during 9-5, but always, when I'm hurting, when I'm scared, when I'm happy.

Just like the T in merlot or the K in know, it may be silent, but it doesn't get removed from the spelling. God sometimes may be silent in mine and your lives, but it doesn't mean He has removed Himself from us.

Deuteronomy 31:8, The LORD himself goes before you and will be with you; He will never leave you nor forsake you. "Do not be afraid; do not be discouraged.

Love

Back on the theme of the royal wedding, I looked at Prince Harry when he met Meghan at the altar and all through the service you could just see him staring at her in admiration and pure love. He was just on love.

It got me thinking, God loves us more than the above scenario, He loves so much more that He gave His ONLY begotten Son to die for us. That's how much we are loved by God. We may not have our bride or groom to look at us with the look of love like Prince Harry and Meghan, we may not have the wedding photographs to reflect the loving ceremony, what we do have however, is a God who was willing to sacrifice His son for us, we have a Son who was willing to be sacrificed, bruised, battered, ridiculed and humiliated, we have a God who gives us His grace and mercy, we have a God who forgives us of our sins, we have a God who provides for us. We have a God whose love will never ever end. In *1 John 4:8 it declares God is love*, God loves us. Sometimes people who get married who were once so in love, end up getting divorced because for various reasons the love has now gone. We have an assurance that God will never stop loving us despite our faults, despite us not living right, despite us neglecting Him. His love is unconditional.

You may think, well, God doesn't love me, let me tell you He does, He declared it *in **John 3:16 For God so loved the world that he gave his one and only Son, that whoever believes in him shall not perish but have eternal** life.* Therefore, that scripture means God's love is inclusive of everyone.

Be blessed today as we reflect, remember and hold on to the truth that God loves us.

Change is coming

A caterpillar is a butterfly who has not realised it yet, this realisation only comes through the process of change, until it goes through the change process it will always remain a caterpillar. A caterpillar was always designed to become something else, it was never to remain a caterpillar.

 It got me thinking, before we became Christians, we were caterpillars, however, once we accepted Christ, we are no longer caterpillars but butterflies in the making. (we are in the process of transformation)

God never designed for us to remain as caterpillars-a caterpillar is slow, moves at a slow pace, does not really do much, can easily be trod on, cannot really see high up, they make look ugly and when we were living in sin, that sin made us look ugly, caterpillars are usually eaten by other animals, and as such Satan is a **_roaring lion seeking who he can devour as found in 1 peter 5:8_**

On the other hand, butterflies on the other hand have a better advantage point, they can fly, reach higher heights, have more movement, it looks beautiful. The same applies to us as butterflies in the making, once that sin is removed from us, we now look beautiful, we can soar high (like wings on an eagle), we are no longer living under people's feet waiting to be trampled on.

We are not fully formed butterflies yet as in *2 Corinthians 3:18 we are being transformed into the same image from glory to glory, we are to be transformed into the image of God.*

Be blessed today as we let God take us through the metamorphic process.

Overflow

A cars petrol tank has the capacity to hold a certain amount of petrol/diesel, once that capacity has been reached, whatever extra petrol/diesel you try and put in the car will just leak out, the same as with a bottle, once it has been filled to its capacity any extra liquid will just spill out. A filled bath will leak out over the sides once full. I could give more examples, but you get my drift. We don't want there to be any overflow. Once we have filled up our car or bath, we use it until it needs refilling again. We are not going to fill a bath with water and then just sit and watch it, we filled it for a purpose, the same with the car, we filled it because we are going to use it. Imagine a bath or sink overflowing, the tap has broken, and you can't stop it and you run around trying to find buckets to contain the overflow of water.

 It got me thinking, when we are asking God to fill us with His spirit, we need to then use it.

As mentioned above we don't want there to be any overflow, but, to me, there are some exceptions, the chorus 'many are the blessings that you give unto me, blessing overflowing like a mighty sea' and 'overflow, let your Spirit overflow'. To me this is saying that I don't want to restrict what God is pouring in to me, I want it, I need it to overflow. I want my cup to runneth over just like in **Psalm 23:5. It states that a cup runs over when it cannot hold all that is being poured into it.** Just think of all that waste running over.

 I want Gods love to overflow in me and in my life. **Psalm 23** shows how gracious and generous our God is, He doesn't provide just enough to fill the cup to the rim, He doesn't limit it to half a cup full, no the CUP OVERFLOWS (not a physical cup). In order to first be filled, we need to empty ourselves of what is not of God. We won't need to be looking for extra buckets to contain the overflow

 I read on the net that we can have overflowing joy, peace.

Be blessed today as you empty yourself in readiness for the overflow

Opposites

Most things have an opposite, light/dark, hot/cold/ fat/thin, tall/small, wet/dry, in/out, good/bad and so forth and it got me thinking, over the years I have felt pretty worthless and I looked at what the word worthless means and it said 'having no real value or use, a person having no good qualities; deserving contempt, without worth; of no use, importance, or value; good-for-nothing' and to be honest that kind of summed me up. I was of no use nor importance to anyone, I offered no value and had no good qualities. Things of no worth generally get thrown away. I felt I had been thrown away with the rubbish, but God looks at me as something valuable, the opposite of worthless is valuable and to be valuable means a thing that is of great worth, having qualities worthy of respect, admiration, or esteem.

 God is saying to me I am valuable, I am of great worth, so much so that He sent His son to die for me. He sees my qualities, they may not all be good, but He is telling me and showing me, I have something good inside of me, He has not thrown me away, He sees my worth. An item that is valuable is taken care of, you don't want to damage it in case it becomes worthless or God is taking care and protecting me. Some people even insure valuable items in the event the item gets lost/stolen etc. God has covered me, He is insuring me. HE WILL NOT LET MY WORTH BE DEVALUED.

Be blessed today, it's a battle but one day I will see and embrace my worth

Let there be....

I was reading **2 Corinthians 6:14** yesterday and it mentioned what **communion has light with darkness?** And it got me thinking, light and darkness cannot work in conjunction with one another, one dispels the other, one counteracts the other, they are opposites not designed to work together, they work independently of each other, they each have a function.

Darkness makes everything black, it's hard to see, can make you feel gloomy, we often say have a dark cloud hanging over us, why not say light cloud? Darkness makes things hard to see or find, but it can also be of aid when you want to sleep, you need the darkness.

Light however brightens things up, we may feel less burdensome, we may say I feel as light as a feather as opposed to feeling dark as a feather. Light enables us to see things, find things, do more things.

For the last couple of days darkness has been my light, it has made the future hard to see, made it hard to find strength, hard to pray or read the bible. I just wanted the darkness to consume me permanently.

 But just like the minute you flick on a switch, light a match, shine a torch, light a candle, darkness immediately goes, it must go, it's been counteracted by another source, even the tiniest light can make a difference.

 I need Jesus to be my light and salvation, I need Him to be a lamp unto my feet and a light unto my pathway. I need the light of the world, the same God commanded let there be light, I need to command in my circumstance let there be light! Easier said than done at the moment

Keep me in your prayer's saints.

In Him and through Him

World Suicide prevention day

In relation to my earlier blog regarding this subject, I just need to let you know that GOD IS ABLE TO BRING YOU THROUGH. He brought me through time and time again. Although the storm may be raging, all storms eventually cease. Trust God, call on Him, cry out to Him. He will hear and answer you.

World Suicide Prevention Day is an awareness day observed on 10 September every year, in order to provide worldwide commitment and action to prevent suicides, with various activities around the world since 2003.

If you feel you are struggling or need help you can contact the Samaritans who are available 24 hours a day, 365 days a year in the following ways:

Telephone 0330 094 5717 or 116 123

In Him and through Him

Printed in Great Britain
by Amazon

66674926R00064